Life should always end up just peachy.

I decided to write a book that bashed my exes. Then I woke up and realized that I did not love myself. I was stuck in a world where everyone could do wrong but me, I did not acknowledge that the world did not revolve around me. After I put my all into the book, I began to feel and see the world from a new point of view. I stopped looking at myself as a victim. Not only in relationships with boys but with my friends and family. Then I started to heal and write about how I view myself now. I treated people so wrong and I always felt like people walked all over me but I also had been walking all over people without and realizing it. I lost sight of reality and was living in my own delusional world. I lost sight of how to be a person who understood empathy. Truthfully, I had completely lost myself. I had to wake up from that blinding life and understand what self-worth was and begin practicing self-love. Living in your own miserable world is useless to self-love and indulging in negativity of any sort is useless to self-worth. I had to accept who I was to become who I am today. I had to find closure in my own faults and in pain caused by others. I am not the person I once was because I have evolved as a human being.

Understand that I have been in and out of relationships and friendships. I have been hurt and I have hurt others. I have learned things and I have learned to unlearn things. I took a huge grasp of reality and learned how to smile again.
Life for me is simply,
Just Peachy.
I am on my own path to self-love.
I am growing and glowing.
This is my life on pages, enjoy.

Just Peachy

God,
Thank you for blessing me with this amazing gift of writing and with the strength to start and finish this book. I put my all into it. For every day I doubted myself, I know you were the reason I never gave up. I would be nothing without God. Thank you.

Ma,
Thank you for pushing me past my limits ever since I was in elementary school. I was placed in daycare at two years old and cried to be moved to the 4's, every day. You had me moved and I never cried again. I watched you walk across the stage twice, for your bachelor and your master degrees. I watched you walk down an aisle in Jamaica and marry the only man I've seen treat you like the Queen that you are. You moved me out of the projects and paved a way for success into the palm of my hands. You've hugged me through sleepless nights, forever making sure I am good. I would be nothing without my mother. Thank You.

Chulo,
Our relationship is one of a kind. You look into my brown eyes, the same color as yours, and find peace. You hold my hand, proud to be responsible for my life. You hug me tight and kiss my cheek with those super wet lips, leaving my heart feeling warmer than before we seen each other. You are my father, my first love, and best friend through it all. You are an amazing parent, loving my every flaw and raising me to your best ability. I would be nothing without my father. Thank you.
Forever, daddy's baby girl.

Just Peachy

Table of Contents

The Why

The Hurt
The Feels
The Now

The Future

The Why

You might not know what you want now. You might not know what you want tomorrow, next month or next year. But deep down, you know what you do not want. Deep down, you know what you will and will not tolerate; you know your limits. At times, we degrade our worth because we think life either can't get any better or can't get any worse. So we settle. I am stressing to every reader who picked this book up, do not settle in a world full of endless options and opportunities. Do not stay in any situation that makes you feel stuck, you are not stuck. This world is as much mine as it is yours, but it doesn't owe you or me a damn thing. So you have to go out and grind to make everything you ever dreamed of happen. A closed mouth does not get fed, remember that.

Dedicated to: the lost girls and boys who just want to be loved, by themselves. Until you love yourself for who you are, no one can truly love you. To the young adults who never even heard of self-love until they were already a senior in high school or freshman in college. To those who don't even know how to define self-love because self-love is not taught in the health class curriculum but how to put a condom on is. This is for the ones that lay in bed at night not knowing that they are great because they don't hear it enough. We all just want to be on top of the world at 17, 20, 22 years old. Unfortunately, life is not that easy, but we are enough, we are all on our own paths running or walking at our own pace.

Ever heard of that saying, "There comes a time when you have to stop crossing oceans for people who won't even jump a single puddle for you"? I got to that point around February 2017. I was consistently crossing oceans and giving my all to too many people. Everyone wants a hundred second chances to just mess them up a hundred times. You allow people in and they take full advantage of you. Not all people, but a large handful do and I think that sucks for people like me. It sucks for people like you who picked up this book. As we get older, we grow more as individuals and realize how selfish and greedy people really are, they take and take but never have the heart to give and give. People tend to get comfortable and expect so much from people like us and we just give it to them, sometimes without even realizing how vulnerable we have become. At times, we might even play the victim role and become the people who we dread and take advantage of others because we have been hurt by our past. But really, how long are you going to carry all of that hurt on your shoulders and expect to move on? My advice, stop exhausting and burning yourself out, unnecessarily.

Love yourself because you are who you are and not as a favor to yourself and you will see the world so much differently.

I sat in the same spot for a very long time. And shortly before I finished writing this book, I still felt like at times I was sitting in that same spot. And that was because I sat there trying to be someone I wasn't for someone who deserved so much more than I could give. I also sat there trying to be someone I wasn't for someone who never deserved me. I conversed with the same group of friends that have been talking about the same bullshit since high school. I've dwelled on the same family problems for years. I've held onto grudges with people who probably haven't thought about me in months. I encourage everyone to let it go. Please, let it go so you can finally grow and glow. You can fix something but you cannot fix someone. No one is broken. No one is fixable.

So as you are reading, I ask that you find it in yourself to begin to forgive those people who intentionally or *unintentionally* hurt you. It will lead to you finding self-love and respecting your worth. Those people took a huge loss when they took advantage of you, thinking that they could under-love you forever. Love, of any kind, is double sided and you do not deserve less than for someone to meet you halfway. And you certainly don't deserve to halfway love yourself. We only live once, we only get today once. Yesterday is gone, it is now the past. Don't run from all of your problems but learn to let go of the ones that won't matter. You will make it through. You will smile again. You will find a new soul mate. You will find a new best friend. You will find yourself again. Learn how to forgive and recover from your situation instead of forgiving and forgetting.

This book is filled with things I have written over the past year. Its filled with my side of the truth, the way I felt and saw things through my own eyes. Thank you for even picking up my book. I hope it changes your idea on how to handle situations. I hope it helps you find self-love or guide you to it. This is my journey. Even if only one line touches you, I'm glad you could relate. That proves, I am not the only one. And my friend, you are not the only one. We are not the only ones.

Self-Love:

To me, self-love is not a form of conceit. It is not narcissism. It is confidence in one's self and acceptance of one's self. Self-love is something you achieve, but can lose if once you achieve it, you stop practicing it. It is an ongoing, everlasting process. Self-love is truly believing that you are good enough, for yourself. It is being whomever you are no matter where you are and who you are around, it is knowing your self-worth. It is loving all of who you are and knowing that when you stop growing as an individual, it is time to re-evaluate your current environment and circumstances, and begin to evolve again. It is self-awareness, being good to yourself. It is being honest with yourself. It is maintaining daily functions, no matter what your current situation is. Once you practice *true* self-love daily, I believe you have built the foundation for the true meaning of happiness.

The Hurt

Just Peachy

I tried to fix myself for you
I contorted myself to please you
sadly,
you never seemed pleased by my efforts.
I had a fragile grip on reality,
truly believing
that someday you would see me, for me.
that someday you could possibly
love me for me.
I was conforming myself to fit another
human being's standard.
and in the end,
it didn't matter that I let you down.
what mattered was that I let me down.
I grew tired of someone devaluing
my love for them.
and we got to a point where it wasn't
anything left for me to say.
and there sure as hell wasn't any more
excuses I cared to hear
come out of your lying mouth.
forget that you never
saw the real in me.
cause you never made a single attempt,
at seeing the real me.
therefore, the love you claimed
to have for me was simply,
all make believe.
I wish you well *man*.

Just Peachy

I am not sure why I stayed,
trying to be someone
that was way out of my character.
from the beginning, you told me
that we would end up at a dead end.
you told me that you already
belonged to someone else
and that we would just be temporary.
you told me that I could never
have you as my own.
you told me that I would never
get the chance to steal you from her.

*clearly you brought nothing
to the table.
silly me for trying to turn
nothing into something.*

*the thing is, in my head, I had already
stolen you from her. because how could you
want me in any way if you already had a
girl? if this girl treated you so well,
how did you have eyes for
just some girl?*

our love story contained two flaws.
one, I was too young to understand
our potential.
and two, you were madly in love
with me.
you never hurt me.
you've been nothing but good to me.
I knew from the beginning that our love
for each other was catastrophic.
or at least,
I was to you.
me, with that selfish mindset.
and you, living in an illusion where
no bad could be formed inside of me.
when in reality
I was the worst thing for you.
how did you not see
that while you were trying
to love me,
I was tearing us down?

blinding yourself with fake love,
we all fall for this fatal mistake.

Just Peachy

it's exhausting,
everyone wanting a part of you.
it makes you feel like you're not even
whole to people anymore.
everyone wants the happy girl but I get
sad too and the second that I do,
no one is there.
everyone I've ever grown to love
has left me for someone else.
it's like I'm not good enough
so I put on this front
like no one else is good enough either.
and I know that if I keep this mentality,
I won't let myself be good enough for
myself.

it's like wearing a happy mask,
every day.

late night phone calls
that I still answer
because I confuse the
hold you have on me
with the love
you never had for me.
I keep wishing
you'd let me go
but I'm hoping
that you'll find it
in yourself
to change for me, for us.
I'll always be your favorite
game to play
where one day you wake up
loving me and
hating me the next.
and I just keep losing myself
trying to save a heart
that was never mine.

Just Peachy

I just needed you to see me.
I tried everything for you to see me.
but you never saw me.
my emotions and thoughts
were too deep for you.
so I damn sure knew,
my love would be too grand for you.
but I kept having this urge
for you to see me.
my mixed up emotions
that were buried in my mind.
and my thoughts
all jumbled up in my heart.
I had no idea how I felt about you,
anymore.
you gave me chills
in the summer.
making me feel heat waves
in the winter.
constantly falling for you
in the spring,
but as usual,
autumn came and your love
never blossomed for me.

*you were the one who made me realize,
people too, are all so seasonal.*

you always come back,
with no intent on loving me.
you want to kill the happiness
that I find without you.
I know that you know that
you don't want me.
but silly me,
I continue to stand there,
always willing to be yours.
oh, the power you hold over me.
my heart, left shattered in the palms of
your fucking hands, every chance you get.
my dear, why do you do this to me
fuck up my heart so much that
I've learned how to tuck my mind away.

*it took some time, but I stopped thinking
that I needed someone that never deserved
me.*

Just Peachy

she fakes all of that confidence.
walking with her head high and chin up.
she is an actress to the world
because she's insecure
with a damaged soul.
but her heart is so big
and her intentions remain pure.

that is how she's learned to survive.

you know I see every ounce of pain,
running through your veins.
it's like you let it all sit there,
as you drink your life away.
it's like someone hurt you,
but you never speak of their name.

that makes you brave,
do you know that?
it makes you fierce.

in murdering you,
they murdered a part of us.
anger filling our hearts some nights.
we never speak of their name because
we don't even know who we're angry at.
please stop killing our own people. *- 609.*

Just Peachy

"you're a baby"

but I can devour your soul.
I look at you and you want more.
sexual tension, on your side.
you keep calling.
and I answer, as a good deed done.
I make your body shake,
in ways that she could never.

I was just a fucked up,
very brief chapter in your life
that you tossed to the side
once you got what you wanted.

"but does she know that?"

Just Peachy

you fell in love with me first.
I just loved for way longer.
you did this to me.
I never wanted to love you.
I felt obligated to.
now I'm stuck in a terrible situation.
you move on first and I love last.

he did not understand how someone who made him feel so warm inside could feel so fucking destroyed.
he said that her eyes remained cold, but her body was heated, filled with victories that she saw as being defeated.

Just Peachy

they beg for you back.
then drag you
through more dirty lies,
hurt you again,
bruise your heart
more than they already did.
they think it's okay
because you never have the
guts to stick up for yourself.
it's their world and
you just live in it,

I just didn't know how to throw my selfish
ways aside for you. egotistically, I
didn't take in that you matter too.

she became just like
the people she dreaded
and hurt the only person
who actually treated her right.
so the words *I'm sorry*
no longer meant a thing
to him, coming from her.

I like to believe that karma
is not real.

Just Peachy

```
you would stroke my hair,
and call me beautiful.
you would laugh at all of my jokes,
and call me amazing.
you would hold my hand,
and call me your forever.

amazingly,
that beautiful day called forever,
finally came and you never looked back
at my beautiful hair
and my amazing laugh
you let go of the hand
you promised forever.
```

you felt my love
consuming your heart
and at the age of seventeen
that was too much for you
to handle.
so you broke my heart
and moved on
with unfulfilled promises to me,
that you would eventually
begin promising her.

Just Peachy

do not reminisce over her.
she gave you her all
and you still left.
maybe she wasn't
your type
or you weren't
ready for her.
but she was more than enough.

you left me for her,
stop searching for me in her.
and don't come back,
searching for her in me.

you made me
lose my self-control
stepping over the truth
that you laid out in front of me
without caution.
a useless factor in my future.
I decided to see
what I wanted to see in you,
that was my fault
when it came time to pinpoint
any kind of disappointment.

do not build a fantasy land out of a
temporary boy just turning into a man.
believe him when he tells you
"I am who I am".

Just Peachy

in attempt
to hurt you back,
I lost a piece of myself
that I didn't even know
was a part of me.
my soul sister,
so I'll always
wish you better
but the betrayal
hit too deep
for me to ever act
like this didn't turn into
the end of
best friends forever.

friends come and go,
and they'll slaughter your heart,
more than *he* ever will.
replacing you,
faster than *he* ever did.

Just Peachy

words I speak
will grab onto your soul.
blunt and to the point.
passionate about proving
all those boys who said
"this is your loss" wrong.
I'll make your heart bleed,
a sickness called:
I need her kind of love back.
but it's one in a million.
trying to remain a simple girl,
who will someday
become my own best friend
in a world full of betrayal.
I have done too much for people
and I can feel the love
will never be returned.
happiness I brought others,
never was reciprocated.
even after realizing
people didn't deserve
my kind of love,
I gave it to them.

I would have moved mountains with people,
but they wanted me to do it all alone.

you shoved the idea
of forever
down my throat
before I ever got the chance
to love myself.
you wanted us to be
in love
before you ever got the chance
to love yourself.

young love.

Just Peachy

masking my beauty
with piles of make up
to sit in *his* house
and he never even noticed.
he only wanted one thing
and it was not my raw beauty
or my enhanced beauty,
it was to use my body
and never take me seriously.

this generation got tricked into believing
that all we need is an instagram woman
crush wednesday post for validation.

my tears were caused
by all of you.
but I woke up
and still smiled,
playing the *I'm just peachy*
role to the world.
and that is how I made
the pain caused by all of you
numb my heart completely.

Just Peachy

when you walked out of the door
for the very last time,
I felt hopeless.
you no longer wanted me.
and that made me no longer want
that version of myself.
you were a part of my every day.
now, I can't go
to our favorite places anymore,
even though a lot of those places
were my favorite
before they were our favorite.
you no longer felt a reason
to love me.
and that made me no longer want
to love that version of myself.
you were my morning, afternoon,
night and everything in between.
I can't imagine receiving
my favorite flowers
from anyone else,
even though those were
my favorite flowers before you existed
in my world.

do you understand the impact you had on me? I didn't change for you, I adapted to you. and now, I have no clue how to be me, without you.

I let go of you
in order to figure me out.
you kept trying to fix me,
while I kept trying
to explain to you
that I was never broken
and even if I was,
I was not your job to fix.

Just Peachy

you look at her
and you can only see greatness.
you think
all of her pieces are put together.
yet, when she looks at herself,
all she sees is a convoluted mess.
she's a young girl,
waiting for her life to blow up
in her own face.
she's been through her own hell
and just hasn't found her way back yet.
she might just need some more time.
are you willing to give her that time?
the time to grow into
the woman you know
she has the potential to be.

God,
please know that I wish him well.
please know that I wish him better.
please know that I wish him joy.
but God,
I also wish he never meets someone better than me.
I don't want him well off without me.
I don't want to see him infatuated with someone else's joy.
God,
I know it's selfish of me,
because I was the one who did wrong.
but I am human and he was once my world, too.

Just Peachy

I do not believe in much,
but I do believe in this:
people who cheat are selfless.
people who cheat are dying inside.
secretly not happy,
but putting on a happy face,
for the person that they *used* to love.
they sneak around to satisfy
another person's feelings because
they still care.
not setting themselves free
to make the other person remain happy.
still exhausting themselves
for someone who claims
to be in love with them,
but can't even see how miserable
they have become.

at least that's what he told me.

chasing someone who does not want you
is exhausting.
being a *little secret*
is not worth the sleepless nights.

*do not try to repair something
that was never made to be put together.*

Just Peachy

your words said you loved me
but your actions said
you just wanted to fuck *(me over)*.
you hated yourself
and took that hatred out on me.
you were great at playing pretend,
in between these female's legs.
I just wasn't sticking around for that.

I might have been hurt a lot,
but I knew I deserved better than that.
my daddy taught me the game
better than that.

laying in that bed with you,
I was trying to make sense of us.
I thought *this is what happens
when you get older.*
but it's not.
you do not get older
and forget your worth
all to be loved
by another human being.

because that is not love.

Just Peachy

I believe that my father
wanted to build me
so that I never viewed myself as broken.
too bad I never took my father's advice
leave those boys alone
and focus on yourself.
the day I escaped from my tower,
I tore down daddy's little princess
all before the age of sixteen.
I began to hate who I was becoming,
daddy's little rebel.

just because I am pretty to you,
does not mean I am pretty to me.
some nights I hate the girl
you think you see.
because underneath all the beauty
you think you see,
the girl inside, is broken.
I hardly recognize myself some mornings.
smiling to the world
because that's what pretty girls are
supposedly, supposed to do.

I am tired of being the pretty girl.
I want to be the smart girl,
with a pen and paper
that lights your whole world up

Just Peachy

The Feels

Just Peachy

after being knocked down
so many times,
she finally began to see
the real in people.
being a genuine person
wasn't working for them.
it seemed to her,
that people wanted a show
and with her fire,
that's what they got.
she sparked the match
on falling bridges
with people who no longer
deserved her energy.

countless times, she's been shown why she should never expect shit from anyone besides the person she stares back at in the mirror and at times that person even lets her down, so she disposed of that fragile girl and she set fire to the hurt girl and began to feel again.

Just Peachy

honesty was obviously something
you never could get
a clear understanding
of how to be with me.
a complete fool
stuck with the torment of being
in love with the idea of you.
you fucked me over
and I would have never expected that kind
of energy from you.
you kept claiming to be from the jungle,
so I let you in whenever you knocked
on my kingdom doors.

Fuck, I kept letting you in.

all I could think about,
dream about,
was you.
you were suffocating me
even after you left me and
broke my dainty little heart.
but today is the day I move on
and I set my mind free of you.
today I will take the first
real breath of fresh air
I've taken in years.

Just Peachy

```
coloring inside of the lines.
I found myself in you.
coloring outside of the lines.
I found myself in me.
```

you left me
and I could finally feel myself again.

once I fell in love with myself
I became a threat to you.
and that is something I'll never
grow to understand.

I just needed to love myself a little bit more to realize all I ever needed was me.

Just Peachy

you were perfection
on a rainy day.
clouding my judgement
of any bad vibe.
you walked into my life
and it feels like a new beginning,
my very own rainbow.
God sent you just for me.
    Forever.

someday, one day
it'll come to me
if I stop searching for it.

I finally saw you again.
your eyes met mine,
you looked like you
could've fallen in love again.
but it wasn't with me this time.
you simply glanced at me,
we simply just met eyes.
and you went back to being with her.
I did all that I could to keep you.
but still, you choose her.

it will always be hard to see the boy who broke you down become the man of another girl's dreams.

Just Peachy

know what disgusted me the most?
you sat there and *lied to her face.*
you sat there and told her that
you love her.
she's this perfect piece
to your fucked up masterpiece.
but come fall,
you told the world I never
learned my lesson.
meanwhile,
you were texting and calling me.
it blew my fucking mind.
and eventually,
I grew tired of being the crazy one.
think you blinded me with your words,
cause it wasn't anything worth
degrading myself for,
in between those dull blue bedsheets.
I would never throw dirt on your name,
but you left me in the dirt.
you left me
to figure shit out on my own
I had to fix my own masterpiece
that you deliberately tore down,
in order to plaster your own.
I crawled into the palm of your hand,
while you had her sitting in the other.
you were controlling what she saw,
while I had to watch
the whole thing play out.
you made me the crazy one.
but I learned my lesson
and I found a way out.

choosing myself
over a falsified love of you
was the best thing
I could have ever done for myself.
I no longer had to deal with
the lies you feed yourself
in order to blurt out
a made up truth to me.

she glows in a new way. do not come back
trying to take all of that new found self-
love away from her in order to boost your
ego, again.

Just Peachy

you made his heart sink
and butterflies filled his chest
every time he saw you.
and that, I'm sure was a great feeling.
but then I came into the picture,
and he knows now that
he could never picture his life
with anyone else.
his heart never even skipped
a beat after that,
there wasn't a need to,
I was right there by his side.
he felt as though he settled for you.
he settled for mediocre
happiness with you.

to me, from his new lover.

baby girl,
focus on yourself.
ignore boy's judgements of you.
they want to mold you
into their idea of a woman
before they even turn into a man.

Just Peachy

```
he needed her to just be there
but she had her own nightmares
casted by her own demons
that she had to face.
she couldn't be your savior too.
```

they all became the same.
vulnerable to my touch.
sensitive to my words.
wanting more than I said I'd give.

for once,
I wasn't the hopeless romantic.

Just Peachy

I asked you why you liked me
and you threw adjectives at me
I told you that was nice but
how do I make you feel
you told me I was doing too much
and dismissed the conversation.

a wasted body, added onto a list of fuck boys.

you said it so sweet and innocent.
whispering to me how much you loved
my body.
I knew it was just to make me feel better
because every night I'd unlock your phone.
more girls.
prettier girls.
with big booties.
and big boobs.
I figured out that I was your safety net.
obviously, to you pussy is replaceable.
so you can leave now.
you can move on to what you really want.
and no it's not your loss.
you got what you wanted.
but when you see me happy with the next,
don't come crawling back,
my stimulating mind and little curves
weren't good enough then,
they won't be good enough now.

Just Peachy

in a relationship
where he never even
took the time to get to know you,
what did you invest in yourself?
what did you get out of all that hurt?

do not be that girl.

I stopped caring
and that confused you
because it was as if
I would never stop
fighting for you.
but even with all
the love I had for you
resting in the pit of my heart,
I knew I would have to
stop giving a fuck
for you to notice
that I mattered too.

I no longer have any intentions
on giving you the kind of attention
you've overlooked for years.

Just Peachy

if I told you that years ago
I would dip my head
in the bath water
and scream to the top
of my fucking lungs,
would you believe me?
would you be able to handle
the fact that the strong girl
you see now,
was once weak too?

in order for me to
love myself for myself
I had to
save myself from myself.

*and that us when the numbness
began to fade.*

Just Peachy

and perhaps it was my fault,
believing that my feelings mattered
to anyone but myself.
believing that my love
could be acknowledged and respected
for what it was.
that my heart would be appreciated.
perhaps I was asking for too much.
or perhaps all this time,
I was too much for you to believe in,
too much for your ego to consume.

it's time to love yourself first.
and become your own kind of great.

I became my own comfort zone.
sitting in a bathtub,
only seeking the attention
from the words spilling
out of my fingertips.

I no longer needed you.

Just Peachy

you were my familiar
but that got boring
and now,
I want to live
on the wild side
where you don't belong
because you like
perfection
and I'm too unapologetic
about who I am
to even care about
what makes you
feel good about me anymore.

I found someone worth letting go
of you for, me.

people wonder why
people like me
just change out of thin air.
as if it was our decision
to get hurt by people we love.
as if we were doing an inhuman thing
by loving the ones close to us.

Just Peachy

you left me,
you moved on.
now you call me.
you're stuck on me,
wanting me next to you.
time to stop the reruns.
I can't be your girl anymore.
can't be your in between.
the here when she's not there.
I can't be your anything.
because,
you made me your nothing.
you turned us into nothing.
this was your doings.
exactly what you said you wanted.
I showed you my worth long ago,
so don't try to realize it now.
I deserve better.
you weren't capable of being better.
I will not sit in the shadows,
of you and her.
I am leaving,
it's my turn to move on.

it is 2:31 am
you are calling to ask if I am happy.
and even if I wasn't,
you left me.
so really
what did my happiness ever mean to you?

nothing.

Just Peachy

I was there then I was here
and that's when I realized
situations change people.
places change people.
people change people.
life changes people.
I realized that
you never really know anyone.

I would not feel secondary.
I would not feel like my stay,
was over stood.
I would not feel like a burden.

*I woke up and felt empty in a full house
and that is when I knew, it was time for
me to go home.*

Just Peachy

broken pieces layered
throughout my body
feeling them,
is so much *different*
than seeing them.
and that is where we
disconnect.
you might hear me,
but you do not feel me.

people tend to come back with the pieces
they stole from me,
as if I want them back,
as if I am the same person from before.

I am not a victim.
I let myself down.
It had nothing to do
with anyone but myself.
stuck in a dark place,
I woke up one summer day
and promised myself
that I would pick
myself back up.

only you can pick yourself back up.

Just Peachy

I find it odd,
girls look at other girls
and feel dislike for them.
when did we allow *society*
to make us this insecure?

I was *pretty for a black girl*
all of my life.
ever thought,
I just wanted to be pretty,
just pretty for me.

Just Peachy

living for you became exhausting.
you pushed me to the edge
and every morning it became:
do I jump and hopefully fly
and find myself or run back
into the comfort of mommy's arms
and continue being
your human redo button.

it took me writing this book to realize
all you ever wanted me to be was great.
I finally jumped and
I've never felt more free,
mommy's twenty year old author.

they want us
to figure the rest
of our lives out
in 720 days.
all to become
a person
we will never be
the second
we walk out of
those doors for the
very last time
on a sunny spring day.

high school.
it is just 720 days.
do not give up on yourself.

Just Peachy

I overlooked all of your fucking flaws
and loved you anyways.
it was so easy for me,
to fall for your charming ways.
but then you got slick
and started lying and cheating.
I fed your ego way too much.
I made you feel like I *needed* you.
so when I finally opened my eyes,
saw your flaws
for exactly what they were
and left,
you were dumbfounded.
as fast as I feed your ego,
I destroyed it with no regrets.

you were rare,
sort of perfect.
too perfect.
and I never wanted
perfection.
I wasn't searching
for a perfect picture.

I have always wanted someone like me,
a beautiful kind of madness.

Just Peachy

if you're bad, I want to be good to you.
I can see through the pain.
I see the wall you've built,
it just doesn't matter to me.
I want to knock that fucking wall down.
the more you push me away,
the more I want to know more.
you're not even a puzzle,
because you're all pieced together.
artwork on the inside,
framed perfectly on the outside.
I don't get why you keep
calling yourself broken.
I see that you can love.
I don't even want that
part of you right now.
just want to hold you tight tonight.
you deserve to be held tonight

"it is not rocket science".
it's not. you're right.
rocket science is rocket science.
anything else is anything else.
I am me.
and she, she's not me.
she's her.
so I don't get why you keep in touch,
after we lost connection
and you found her.
I don't get how you confuse the two of us.
It is not rocket science.

Just Peachy

I cannot conclude this any better
than I can explain it.
how someone I have only touched
bare fingertips with,
made me feel alive again.
then I never saw you again.

thank you for just being you.

*if I would've met you in my 20s,
I would've married you.*
lying words that you used in order
to keep me trapped
in a fucked up situation,
in fake ass happy land.

*shame on me for letting you fool me,
 more than twice.*

Just Peachy

what if I just let you go?
giving you exactly what you wanted.
you've been threatening me for so long,
telling me how easy it would be
for you to let me go.
so let me make it easy for you.
let me let you go,
let me leave you.

or would that mean me having too much control?

if you ever pick this book up,
understand that I no longer hate you.
I feel no ounce of hatred in my bones.
I no longer long for your love,
understand that for once
this isn't about you.
I found the real me and
this is to set her free.
I grew up and finally let you go,
that was the best decision of my life.
understand that you had me tied down
to nothing for too long,
and I figured out how to escape.
understand that we were never meant to
coexist in the same world.
if you ever pick this book up,
understand that you looking
in that mirror every day
and falling into self-hatred
will never be something I allow
this version of myself to be again.

welcome to my twenties

Just Peachy

The Now

Just Peachy

dear old me,

it feels better that I got to success
through a wall of failure.
if I never fell down,
how would I know how it felt
to get back up,
all by my fucking self.
many late nights,
I thought to myself
that I would never see
this side of life.
but failure after failure,
unexpected success had to be coming.
I had to stop looking back,
searching for the girl
who got silver spooned
by not just two, but four parents.
and once I never looked back, at you,
life got so much better for me.
I had to let go of
the spoiled brat act.
especially a spoiled brat
that swore she knew it all.

Just Peachy

```
you always hear
that it's okay
to be the one that
loves a little more
but it's also okay
to be the one that
loves just a little less.
it's okay
to love the world
a little less
in order to love yourself
just a bit more.
```

it's okay.

there is a difference,
instagram happy is not real life happy
and if you're living to show out,
you aren't really living.
paying three thousand dollars
for trips overseas,
just to post it on instagram.
take that three thousand
and invest it into your dreams,
see how much *the gram* cares then.

social media is a wasted,
time consuming, competition.

Just Peachy

she was the perfecting icing
to your cake.
the baker's favorite batter.
everyone wanted a piece.
she was everything you'd never
want to stop tasting.

it wasn't that I thought
I was better than you,
I think I just became
too much for you
and truthfully,
that will never be my fault.

Just Peachy

you are worth more than
what they make you out to be.
repeat that. remember that.
before you go back
to old wounds
that do not deserve
your kind of love back.

turns out that the grass
isn't greener on the other side
and I really couldn't
be happier because
I see a part of me
no one has ever took the time
to see and I found myself
in the midst
of so much bad energy,
the only great vibe
making me smile,
so effortlessly.

I finally looked past the sad girl in the mirror.

Just Peachy

```
you wanted me to be okay with
you loving her,
while loving me.
you're supposed to have your cake,
and eat it too.
but you tried to be greedy,
and eat two.
```

you filled my heart up
with emotional bullshit
about things you never meant
and expected me to stay
accustomed to that empty lifestyle.

I am so happy I got away.

Just Peachy

accept me for me
or leave me for me,
but I will not change myself
for no boy.
no, not again.

I was hurt and then I met *you*.
you'll probably never pick this book up.
but I want you to know this poem is
for you and only you.
we weren't perfect for each other.
but we searched for peace
in each other's eyes.
we have both been through
two different hells.
and for a little while,
we saw eye to eye.
we lived in our our own heaven on earth,
even if it just was
for a little while.

thank you for leaving without a trace,
because of you
I learned how to find closure
in my own space.

the longest relationship
you'll ever have
is with yourself.
work on that first,
make sure that one is always working
towards its happily ever after.

eventually, you have to be yourself and stop trying to find yourself.

you know who you are.
it is time to accept who you are.

Just Peachy

how long will you sit in your own skin,
envying these people on social media?
how long will you wish for someone else's
life when God gave you your own?

wake up every morning and thank God. live to prove yourself wrong and prove God right. this is God's doings; he knew your plan before you made the blueprint. this is God's work; he knew you could do it before you even thought of doing it. he woke you up so you can smile your biggest smile and laugh your loudest laugh. he gave you this time in his world to be someone. so love yourself, always.
we never know the day that our twenty four hours will be cut short.

Just Peachy

you made me feel alive again.
the way you made me smile
turned into the way
you could only make me moan
and fuck, you take my soul away.
I know you'd choose me over anyone else,
I can see it in your stormy eyes.
I get you through hell
and bring you back to reality
with just one smile.
how could you defeat me,
if all you want to do is lust
over my perfectly sun kissed skin.
I glow all over your terrible days
so you can't help but to
fall in love with me.
I fuck with your mentality
but I set you free from the image
they all have painted you to be.

there is a void in your heart,
filled with denial.
allow me to release that void.
you were actually settling for me.
so understand that this is me,
setting you free.

Just Peachy

he came into my life
when no one else
made much of any sense.
so when they asked me
what I saw in him,
it wasn't easy to explain.
all I know now is that he looked
at the deepest and most hurt parts
of my soul and *pretended*
to fall in love with me.
blinded, all I cared about
was that he was there
when the rest of the world
turned their back on me
and I appreciated that the most.
I appreciated that he saw all of me,
for exactly who I was
and still called me beautiful.
he let me know that I was allowed
to fill the places that
they all hurt me at, with gold.
even the places where
he would eventually hurt me.
so when he left,
I felt *vacant* all over again.
I had allowed another person
to consume me.

I realized in that moment,
I had to make myself feel golden.

take care of yourself.
spiritually. mentally.
physically. financially.
just take care of yourself.

cause baby girl, nobody else will.

Just Peachy

guns don't pull their own triggers.
people pull the trigger.
people kill people.
so whoever decided
to pull the trigger on you,
I hope they know
that your life was bigger
than a chain to sell
or more cliental.
it was bigger than
street status and money.
you deserved more than
a bullet to the head
and bullet to the chest,
either one killing you instantly.
we deserved more than to lose our rock.

*you are a legend.
RIP Bubbles, 609.*

Just Peachy

```
being liked
by society
isn't even realistic.
```

figure out what makes you happy
and go for it, with full force.
never look back.

I used to believe that
you were just clumsy with my heart,
incompetent when it came to loving me.
but it wasn't that, at all.
you were just incredibly too stupid
to ever understand how to love me,
it had nothing to do
with your lack of skill set in love
or that we met too young.
so now I know,
it wasn't me at all,
it was always you.

Just Peachy

you love like it is the
last thing you'll
ever be good at.

I'm here to tell you, it's not

we tend to pay attention to lies
because they *sound good.*
when really all we are doing
is robbing our hearts from the truth.
we recognize that we are unhappy
but we stay because we hope.

stop hoping for what was, to come back.

Just Peachy

you asked me not to incorporate you in my
"*dumb writing shit*".
well here is your page.
I no longer have shit to say.

empty, *exactly how you made me feel.*

Just Peachy

stop wasting your time coming up
with apologies for things
that you didn't do,
trying to rekindle a dead friendship.

surround yourself with people
that are on their own paths,
the slightly crazy ones
that all believe in good energy
and great vibes.
people who all want to succeed
and move on to bigger
and better things.

real friends till the very end.

Just Peachy

```
the boy across the street will always be
the boy across the street, priceless.
```

you will get over
the pain of your love
not being what she wanted.

Just Peachy

```
they're always coming back
to what they claimed
to be leaving behind.
```

those are the weak ones,
not you.

after I left you,
I drowned myself in sorrow.
after I realized
I wouldn't be asked to return,
I buried myself in between the words.
then I burned my first book to flames,
because I was over the self-pity party.

Just Peachy

```
some people
are so badly hurt
that they become cruel.
they want to find
their happiness
and then store it in a box
and never share it
with the world,
as if that is real happiness.
```

*do not get sucked
into that world of misery.*

do not stay for the kids.
the kids see your pain.
the kids want to see you happy,
not dying inside.

maybe one day, you too will gain sanity.

Just Peachy

this generation
loves with limits.
we are scared
of getting our hearts broken.
so we love
with the mindset
that eventually,
we are going to get hurt.
and when you love like that,
you are not loving at all.

I was loving myself
as if I was doing myself a favor.
now I love myself unconditionally
because I love who I have become.

no one can take the love I have gained for myself away.

Just Peachy

I wanted to be poetry.
I wanted to indulge in myself.
so that is what I did.
and it finally wasn't about
what they thought.
and it finally became about
what I believed.

there are parts of me
still waiting to forgive
not only the rest of you
but the rest of me.

I had to learn how to
fight for myself
while learning how to unlearn
how to play the victim role.
I defeated all of those demons,
even the demons
that lived inside of me.
I prayed to God to show me
what was for me,
would never pass me.
so this book is proof,
for the ones like me,
now you can feel again
and survive the hurt.
you can let go of the days
that they say make or break you,
because you have thousands more
to become the real you,
to become whomever you choose to be
in this life,
because this life is yours.

so many thoughts
are buried in this book.
maybe one line touched you.
all of them have touched my bare skin,
under all four season's sun.

the best is yet to come.
Stay Peachy.

The Future

As I come to the end of Just Peachy, I hope everyone knows, I gave this book my all. I put my heart and soul into this book. I put my life out into the world, hoping someone can learn from my experiences. I hope everyone finds self-love, it will be the most difficult and rewarding thing you find in your lifetime. I am still working on finding my own version of self-love and this is my journey to it. Writing has been such an amazing experience for me and I found my passion and purpose. Life is too short to drown yourself in your past. So I have learned to write about it until I can't write about it anymore and then, I simply let it go.

There was a time in my life where I felt like I had to prove to the world that I was so fucking tough. I had my walls built sky high and my ego was filled with all of the wrong things. That was back in high school, I thought I was the shit. Then on my first day of college in Georgia, I sat down in my psychology class and my professor said, "I will not remember any of your names. I will call on whoever I want at random because I don't know any of your names". I realized then, no one really gives a fuck about you unless they love you. And in order for anyone to love you, you cannot walk around this world thinking you're some kind of untouchable person that everyone should know and worship. It does not matter how beautiful or handsome you are, if your soul is ugly, you are an ugly person. I am not saying that you shouldn't be confident but feeling like no one can touch you, is just unrealistic and foolish. There will always be someone who possess more beauty than you do, someone with a higher intelligence level, someone naturally better at the sport you train hours a day trying to perfect. There will always be better, but being the best version of ourselves is what we should aim for. That is what self-love is to me. High school was a very low point in my life and it is where a huge part of my anger stems from. I didn't give high school the best version of myself. I was a pretender, trying to be this tough girl, when if you ever had an actual conversation with me, you were able to see right through the act. I have always been very sensitive. In ninth grade a girl wrote a nasty facebook status about me that was not true at all. And that was when high school changed for me. I would not be vulnerable and leave my walls down, so I became a *mean girl*, thinking that would protect my feelings. All because of one post and then a second post at the end of the year of a me tagged in a photo of a horse and people saying "nay" as I walked down the halls, I changed. I became the girl no one wanted to talk to because I was hurt and for four years I viewed myself as a victim. I learned the day of graduation when I had only three friends to take pictures with because literally,

Just Peachy

90% of my senior class disliked me, that I made a fool of myself. I went crazy over two boys that I meant nothing to in high school. I was mean to a handful of females that honestly did nothing to me. I was rude to multiple teachers and was kicked out of classes for various reasons every day. I was a lame. It is not *cool* to walk around saying, "that's just my face". Life is much bigger than you and I think everyone has to learn that before they make the decision to love themselves and become the best version of themselves.

I am 20 years old and this is my first book. I have learned so much through writing this book. I have gained incredible relationships and lost relationships that meant the world to me this past year. But, I am at a happy place in my life right now and no one can steal my joy. No one can take advantage of me or under-love me any longer. I've accepted the hurt I have put upon others and others have put upon me. That is a part of self-love, acceptance. In order to move on and be happy, you have to understand that life is what it is and we only have control over our own actions.

This generation lacks the feeling of empathy; we shrug off other people's problems if we cannot relate. I want my generation to find the willpower to have empathy for others. My theory is that we all are in one huge competition with one another. When if we were to stop comparing ourselves to people we see on social media, we could all be our own kind of great. If we focused on what we want from our time on Earth, we could actually become just that. But we all, at some point or another, bring our peers down and feed into the negative side of social media. There is a huge disconnect within my generation when it comes to reality and social media. I believe if we fill that gap with empathy, *not sympathy,* we can evolve as individuals. If we put our phones down while we hang out with our friends instead of posting every detail of our lives on social media for people who couldn't care less or only want to see us fail, we can evolve as individuals. The ability to experience the feelings of another person (without being judgmental and/ or feeling envious or jealous) is what empathy is to me; that is how we will begin to connect with each other instead of competing with each other.

Thank you to everyone for joining and supporting my journey.

And for my Peachy Babes who have supported me through this whole process, I love you all.

Just Peachy

Thank you Rems for reading my book while it was in the works and honest. I appreciate you on so many levels because you never once sugar coated anything about the book. You are one in a million! I love you.

Thank you Tyra and Tiana for always pushing me outside of my comfort zone. Your stories are forever an inspiration to me.
I love you both, my favorite cousins.

Thank you Krissy for believing in me, always. You have been my role model and have supported me since I was in the 9th grade, I owe so much of my growth to you. I love you sis.

Thank you Jae for being one of my realist and most supportive friends since the first day of high school. It's a May 12th thing, a Chy and Jae thing. I love you.

Thank you Jem for being supportive of my writing since day one. you saw something in me from the beginning and told me I would be an author and now, I finally am. I love you.

Thank you Zani for being my friend since before we knew that we were friends, my annoying big little brother. I love you.

Thank you Kyrin and Zay for being my big brothers and my protectors. I love ya'll.

Thank you Johnny, for literally everything.
I love you.

Thank you to my family and everyone who supported my journey and believed in my vision from the very beginning.

www.ingramcontent.com/pod-product-compliance
Lightning Source LLC
Chambersburg PA
CBHW070159100426
42743CB00013B/2975